MORDY FERBER

COMPOSITIONS

MB22154

Visit us on the Web at www.melbay.com or www.billsmusicshelf.com

Contents

Introduction,

This book is an attempt to capture the highlights of twenty-eight years of composing. Each of these compositions is an expression, and as such -- an exposure, of a genuine part of myself which I present within the framework of jazz; my beloved art form.
When I listen to this music I hear shades of my early classical and rock influences. It also brings to my mind my birth place, a small neighborhood outside of Haifa, Israel.

I really hope that you will listen to these pieces come alive on my CDs   *"All The Way To Sendai"* *Mr.X"* *"Being There"*, and on my next CD due out in 2010. The tunes for TV and film can be found on *www.Mordyferber.com.* You may also want to check out my previous Mel Bay DVD release: *"Make the Tune your Best Friend"* which is a great guide to mastering the performance of a piece of music."
To get the most out of playing these compositions I think you should try them first by yourself until you have the melody and harmony down,
and then play them with other musicians or your band.

Remember, the deeper you search, the more you find.

Mordy Ferber

Foreword

"My most engraved Mordy Ferber memory as an Improvising musician was when I heard him in California with Danny Gottlieb and Jeff Berlin. Mordy's playing was hard-edged, avant-garde, don't give-a damn-about convention and rythmically on fire. This is the spirit of what I like best about Mordy--he chooses hip scale-dissonance coupled with a rebellious freedom that reveals the pure joy of improvisation. As A composer, Mordy shows another side, a more abstract, melodic, original, out-of -the-mainstream approach to jazz and That's the Mordy Ferber to whom no one else can compare...I recommend this book to all music lovers"
Larry Coryell

"Mordy is a wonderful musician who digs deep in his writing and playing with a clear sense of communicating to the listener."
Dave Liebman

All The Way To Sendai

Mordy Ferber

All The Way To Sendai

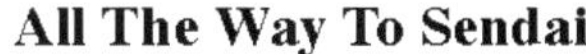

All The Way To Sendai

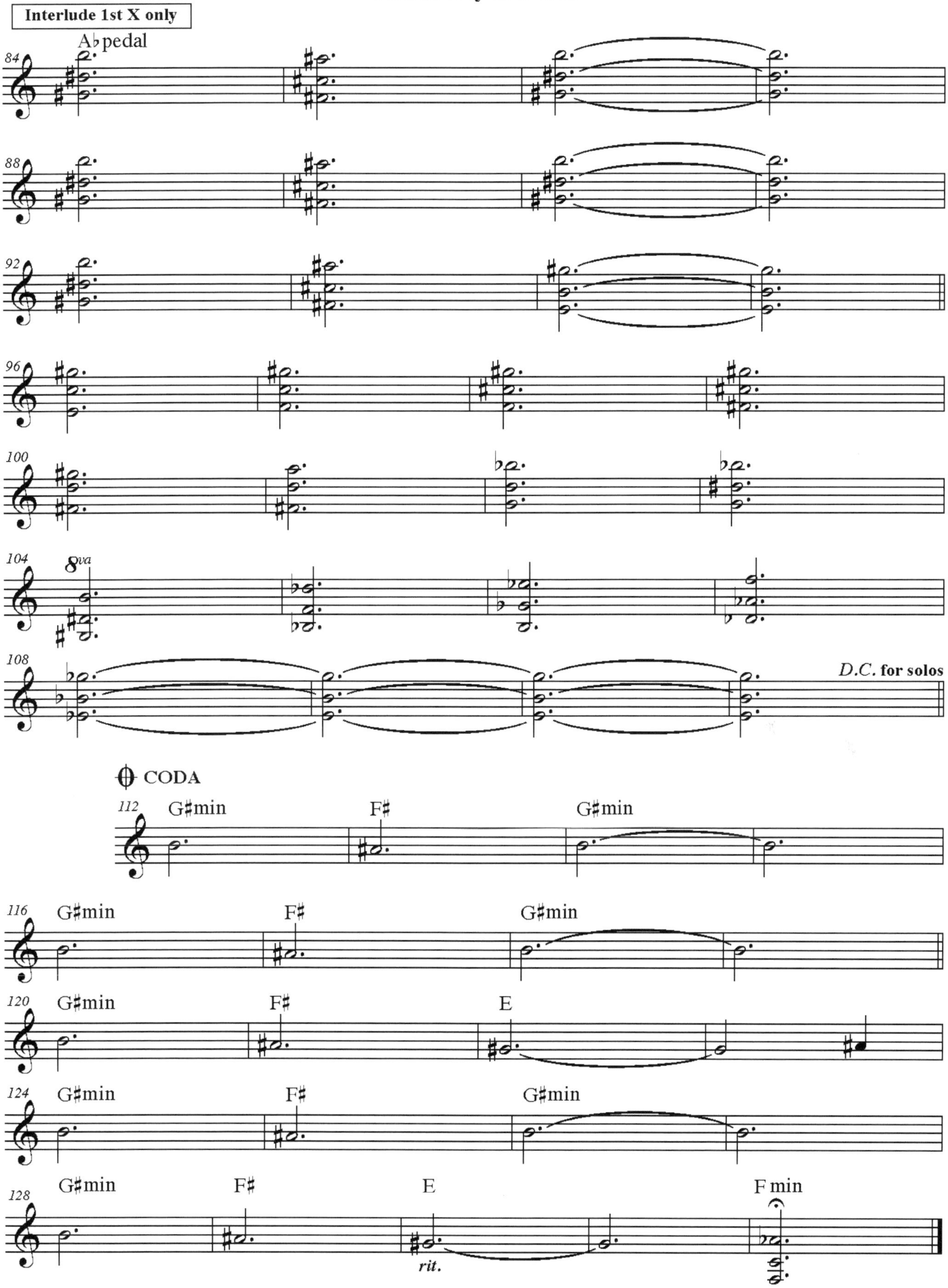

Zipora

Mordy Ferber

Zipora

EMaj9/C
Bbmin7(b5)
B7sus(add3)   A7(#11)
3
Dbmin11/Ab
C7sus4
B7sus4
(Play last time only)
3
3
A min
FMaj7(#11)/A
Bbadd9(#11)
1
E7alt.
to Interlude
2
E7alt.
last time to Coda
INTERLUDE (1st time only)
3
3
3
3
FMaj7
D.C.
for solos
CODA
rit.
rit.

Charlesgate Op. 50

Mordy Ferber

A min/C
A min/B B7
G min/B♭
G min/A
A7
F min/A♭
F min/G G7
D♭Maj7(#11)
C min D♭Maj7(#11)
C min D♭Maj7(#11)
C min D♭Maj7(#11)
1.
F#min7 GMaj7(#11)
A♭min7 4x
GMaj7(#11) 4x
A♭min7 4x
GMaj7(#5) 4x
B♭/C 2x
A7sus4 2x
B♭/C 2x
FMaj7(#5) 2x
B♭/C
B/C#
D.S. back to A
2.
F#min7 GMaj7(#11)
C min D♭Maj7(#11)

SOLO (open)
(Double X Feel)
On Cue
70
C7alt.
Bb/C
Ab/C
Csus2
75
F#dim7/C
Fmin/C
Csus2
SOLO (open)
(Double X Feel)
On Cue
79
C7alt.
Bb/C
Ab/C
Csus2
84
F#dim7/C
Fmin/C
1.
Csus2
2.
D/C
89
CMaj7(#5)
Bbmin/C
Bbdim/C
AbMaj7(#5)
94
Ebmin11
Cmin11
Ebmin11
F#min11
98
Ebmin11
Cmin11
D.S. al Coda
B/C#
D.S. al Coda
CODA
102
Fmin7
Cmin
DbMaj7(#11)
a tempo
3
3
Cmin
DbMaj7(#11)
3
108
Cmin
DbMaj7(#11)
3
F#min7
GMaj7(#11)
rit.

A Minor Tune

Mordy Ferber

A Minor Tune

A Minor Tune
A
37 A min9
GMaj7(#5)
41 CMaj7/G
D7/F#
45 G min7   FMaj7(#5)   A min7   Eb7(#9,b13)   E7(b9,b13)
B
51 A min9   Eb7(#11)   D min7   E min7
55 AbMaj9   BbMaj9
59 B min11   B min11(b5)   E(b9,b13)
63 A min11   G min11   A min11   G min11
67 F#min11
(for ending, vamp on F#min11)
Fine

A Minor Tune

SOLOS
71
A min9
GMaj7(♯5)
75
CMaj7
D9/F♯
79
G min7
FMaj7(♯5)
A min7
E♭7(♯9,♭13)
E7(♭9,♭13)
85
A min7
E♭7(♯11)
D min7
E min7
89
A♭Maj9
B♭Maj9
93
B min11
B min11(♭5)
E7(♭9)
97
A min11
G min11
A min11
G min11
101
F♯min11
D.S. after solos

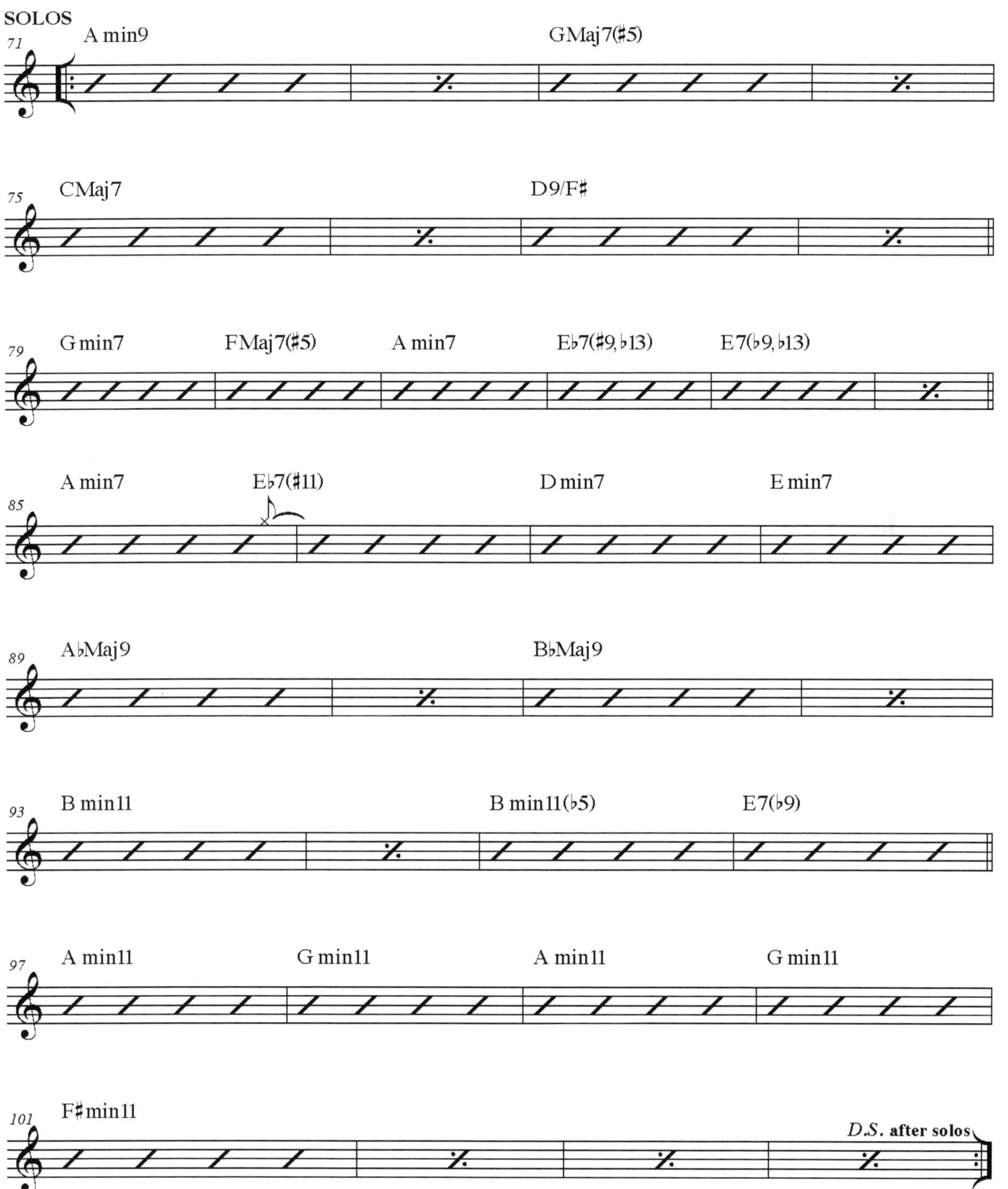

Monolitos

Mordy Ferber

21
Bb7sus(add3)
(bass walks)
Ab13
Gb13
C7(#11, no3)
C7sus4
3
3
>
26
Emin7
(bass walks)
Ab7sus
D7(#9)
C7(#9)
A/B
30
B/C#
F#Maj7(#5)
>
34
EbMaj7(b13)
Ebmin11(b13)
Bmin7
A Phryg.
(bass walks)
D/Bb
D/Bb
3
3
3
3
3
3
39
Freely
BMaj7(#11)
F#Maj7(#11)
Freely (cymbal colors)
3
3

43
Db7sus4
Groove (straight 8ths)
D7alt.
G7(b13)

47
Cmin9
Swing (bass plays figure)
Fmin11
Cmin9
Dbsus/Ab
(Fine)

SOLOS
51
C/D
B/Db
Bb/C
F#7alt.

55
FMaj9
E7
EbMaj9
D7(#9)
DbMaj9
Abmin7

1.
DbMaj7
C7(#9)
BMaj7
Abmin7
2.
DbMaj7
D.C. al fine
after last solo
Dmin7(b5)
G7alt.
61

65
Cmin9
Fmin11
Cmin9
Dbsus/Ab

69
Cmin9
Fmin11
Cmin9
Dbsus/Ab

Fred Astaire in Chicago

Mordy Ferber

Fred Astaire in Chicago
Dbmin7
C7sus4
FMaj7
DbMaj9
BbMaj9
GbMaj9
F6,9
E7alt.
Amin7
Bmin7(b5)
E7(b9)
Amin7
Bmin7(b5)
E7(b9)
Amin7
Bbmin7
Eb7
AbMaj7
Db/Eb
AbMaj7
Db/Eb
AbMaj7
G7(b13)
CMaj7
AbMaj7
FMaj7
DbMaj7
CMaj7
C7
FMaj7
DbMaj7
BbMaj7
GbMaj9
Gmin11
C7alt.
last time to Coda
rit. (for ending only)
Fsus4
D.C. for solos
CODA
F7(#9,#11)/B
21

Mr. X

Mordy Ferber

Solos on Cmin7
After solos D.C. al Coda

Song For Mitzi

Mordy Ferber

This page has been left blank
to avoid awkward page turns.

Formerly With No One

Mordy Ferber

INTERLUDE (before 1st solo only)

Solos on Form
No Interlude on Solo form
Head out: 1x only

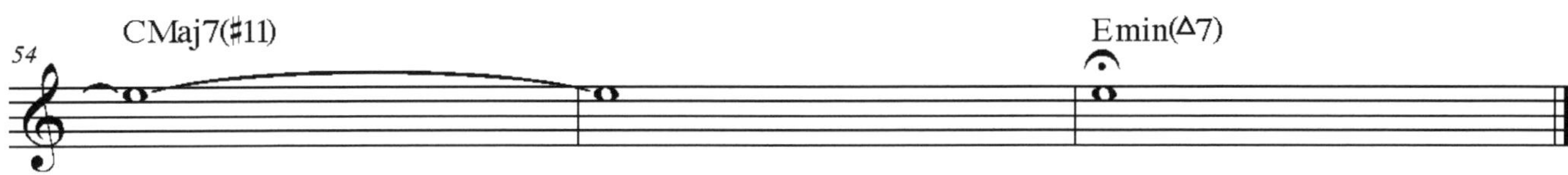

Into the Light

Mordy Ferber

2, 3
B min11(add9)
Bb(#11, add9) A min11 Ab7(#9, b13)
GMaj 13
FMaj7(#11) F#(add4)
F#min/B
F#min/B
B
Cmin7
Abmin7
GMaj
EMaj
Fmin7
C9(#11)
C#min7
A min7
AbMaj
FMaj

Into the Light
F#min7
Melody
Gmin7/F
rit.
FMaj7(#5)
Harmony
rit.
Straight 8ths
BbMaj7(no5)/D
DMaj7
BbMaj7/D
DMaj7(#5)
a tempo
mp
Gb(add9)/Bb
B min7
f
F7(#9)
EMaj9
Eb7(#9)
DMaj9
Db7(#9)
CMaj9
rit.
(Fine)
F#7sus(add3)
a tempo
to Solos
SOLOS (open)
B min11
GMaj13(#11)
D.S.
(last time)

This page has been left blank
to avoid awkward page turns.

Being There

Mordy Ferber

Ballad
F#min   D7(#11, no3)   F#min   D7(#11, no3)
Dmin6   3   F#min11   GMaj7(#11)   3   Db7(b9)
F#min   D7(b5)   F#min   3   D7(b5)
Dmin6   F#min11   Bb/C   Db6   Bb/C   3
CMaj7(#5)   Bb/C   Db/Eb   A7sus(b9)   F#/G
Bmin9   Bmin(△7)/A#   Bmin/A   Bmin6/G#   Amin   Amin(△7)/G#   Amin/G   Amin6/F#
FMaj7   DbMaj7   BbMaj7   Ab/Gb   F/Db
F#min   D7(b5)   F#min   D7(b5)   Dmin6   3

36
F#min11
GMaj7(#11) Eb7(#9)
Ab7
Db7(#9)
Gb7
3
41
F/Db
F#min7
D7(b5)
Db7alt./F
45
F#min
Db7alt./F

1369

Mordy Ferber

F#sus
SOLO
B/C#
C/F#
C#/F#
C/F#
B/F#
1.
2.
to Coda

54
57
61
65
F#min
SOLO (open)
On Cue
68
72
76
F#sus4
bass walks
A7sus4
Emin7(b5)
80
Bb7sus(b9)
G13
E13
G13
E13
1. 2.
84
3.

SOLO Ebmin7
Dmin7
F#sus4 4x
A9sus4
A7sus(b9)
Bb7sus(b9)
G13
Bb7sus(b9)
G13
E13
G13
D.S. al Coda
D.S. al Coda
CODA
drums fill

Rabin

Mordy Ferber

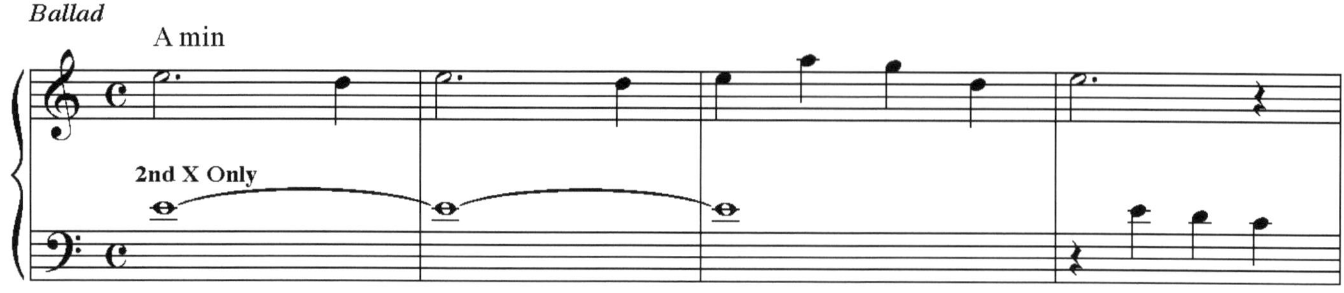

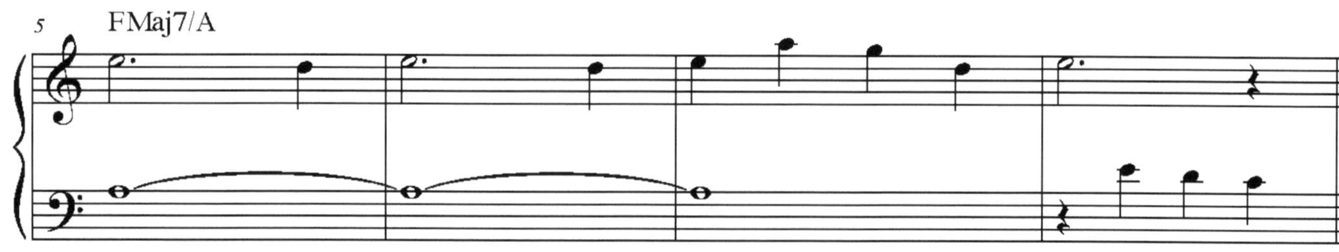

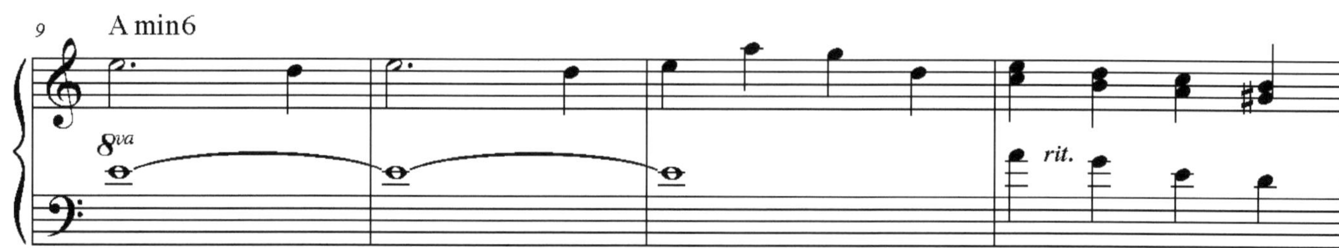

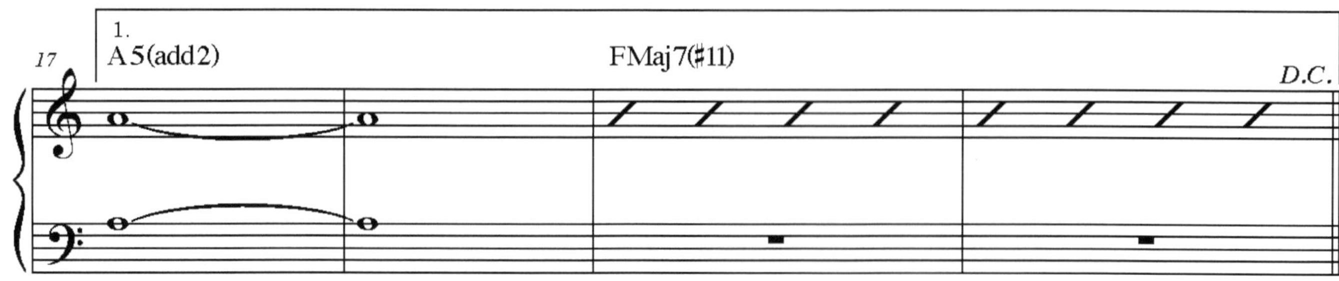

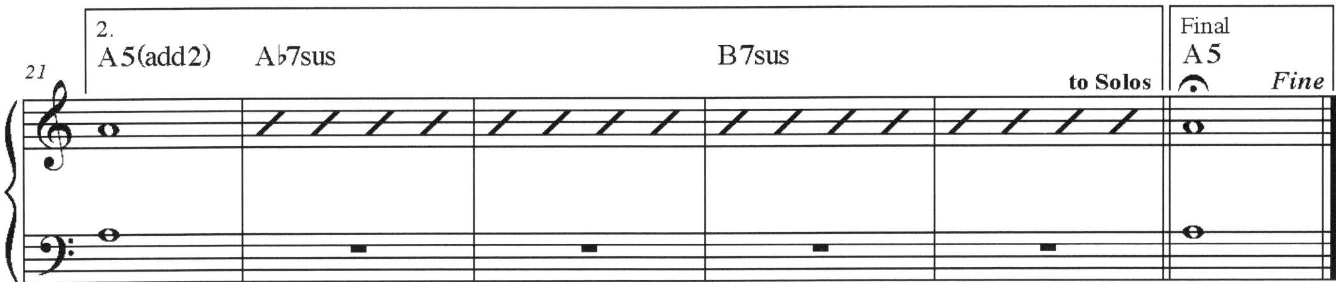

Open solos free time;
Bass solo on cue

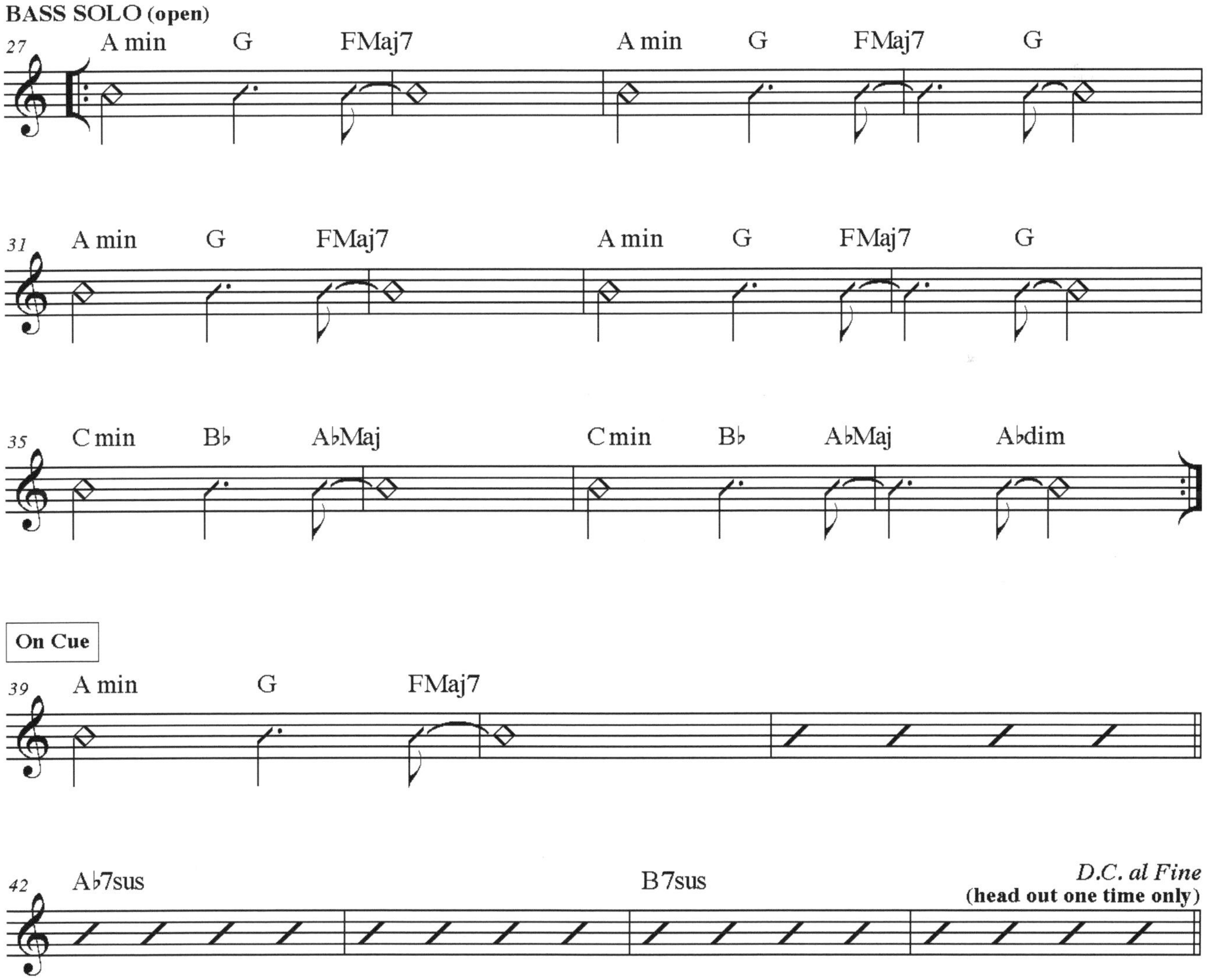

BASS SOLO (open)

On Cue

Wait 'Till You Get Your Supply

Mordy Ferber

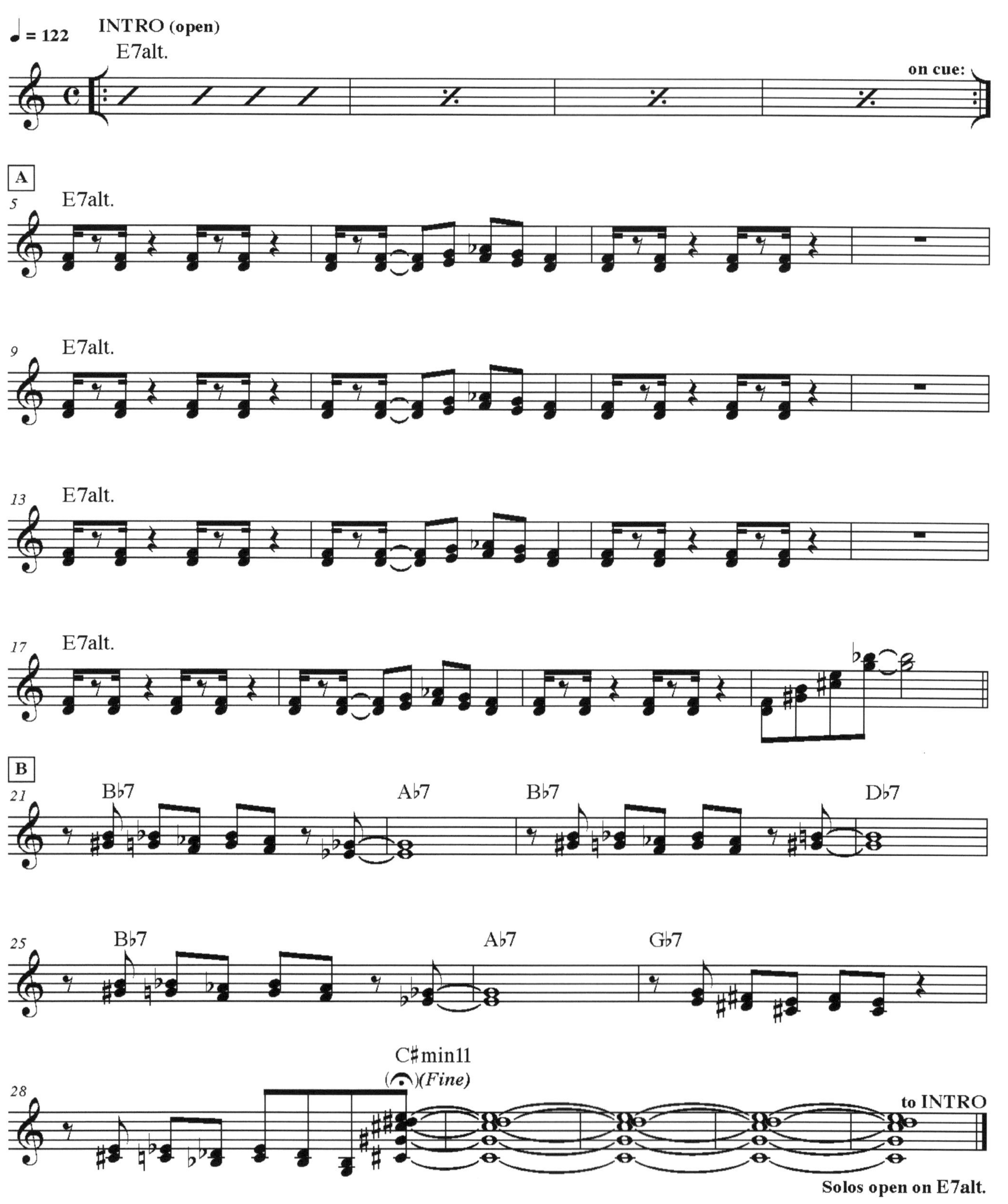

Israel On My Mind

Mordy Ferber

C
28
4X
B min9
B min9
31
B min9
GMaj7/B
35
C7(#11)
3
C#min11
DMaj7
D#min7
D/E
3
39
CMaj7(#11)
43
BbMaj7(#5)
GMaj7(#5)
EbMaj7(#5)
SOLOS (open)
46
E min7
CMaj9(#11)
D.S. al Coda

CODA
SOLO (open)
B min9
On Cue
B min9
3X
B min9
GMaj7/B
C7(#11)
C#min11
DMaj7
D#min7
D/E
CMaj7(#11)
B♭Maj7(#5)
GMaj7(#5)
E♭Maj7(#5)
E min7
(open)
CMaj9(#11)
on cue:
Fine
B min11
rit. (last time)

Farewell Friend

Mordy Ferber

SOLO
43 E min7   D/F#   GMaj7
47 E min7   D/F#   GMaj7
51 F#min7   GMaj7   B min7   GMaj7
55 Abmin7   C#7   C#7(b9)
59 DMaj7   DMaj7   D.S. al Coda
CODA
63 DbMaj7   Abmin7
67 DbMaj7   Abmin7   A 7(#11)
71 Abmin7   Gmin7 Gbmin6   B 7   EMaj7   E min7   A 7
75 DMaj7   GMaj7   DMaj7   GMaj7   DMaj7   GMaj7   DMaj7
82 GMaj7   DMaj7   GMaj7   DMaj7   GMaj7   DMaj7   GMaj7   B min9
rit.

Cinema Kamari

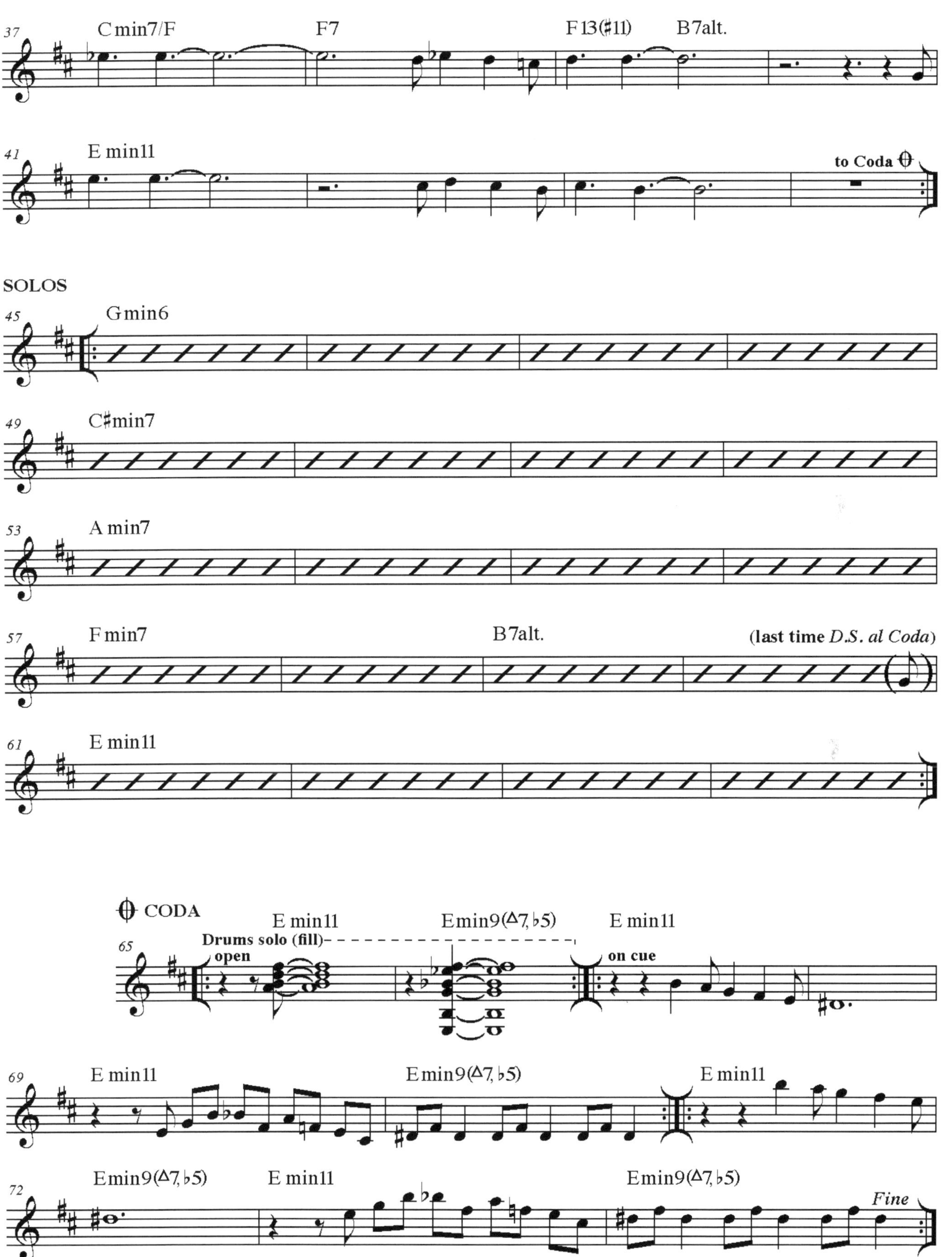

Cinema Kamari
37 Cmin7/F   F7   F13(#11)   B7alt.
41 Emin11   to Coda
SOLOS
45 Gmin6
49 C#min7
53 Amin7
57 Fmin7   B7alt.   (last time D.S. al Coda)
61 Emin11
CODA
Emin11   Emin9(Δ7,b5)   Emin11
65 Drums solo (fill)
open   on cue
69 Emin11   Emin9(Δ7,b5)   Emin11
72 Emin9(Δ7,b5)   Emin11   Emin9(Δ7,b5)   Fine

Grandmother Walks On Whole Tones

Mordy Ferber

Solos open over "A"
Then *D.S. al fine*

Harpo

Mordy Ferber

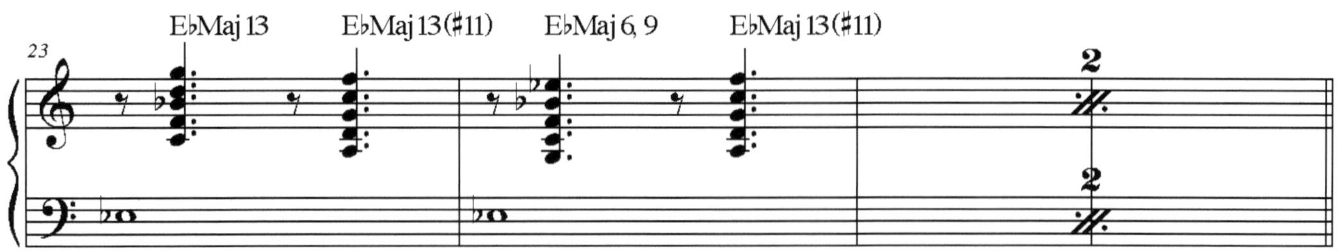

*low E string = E♭

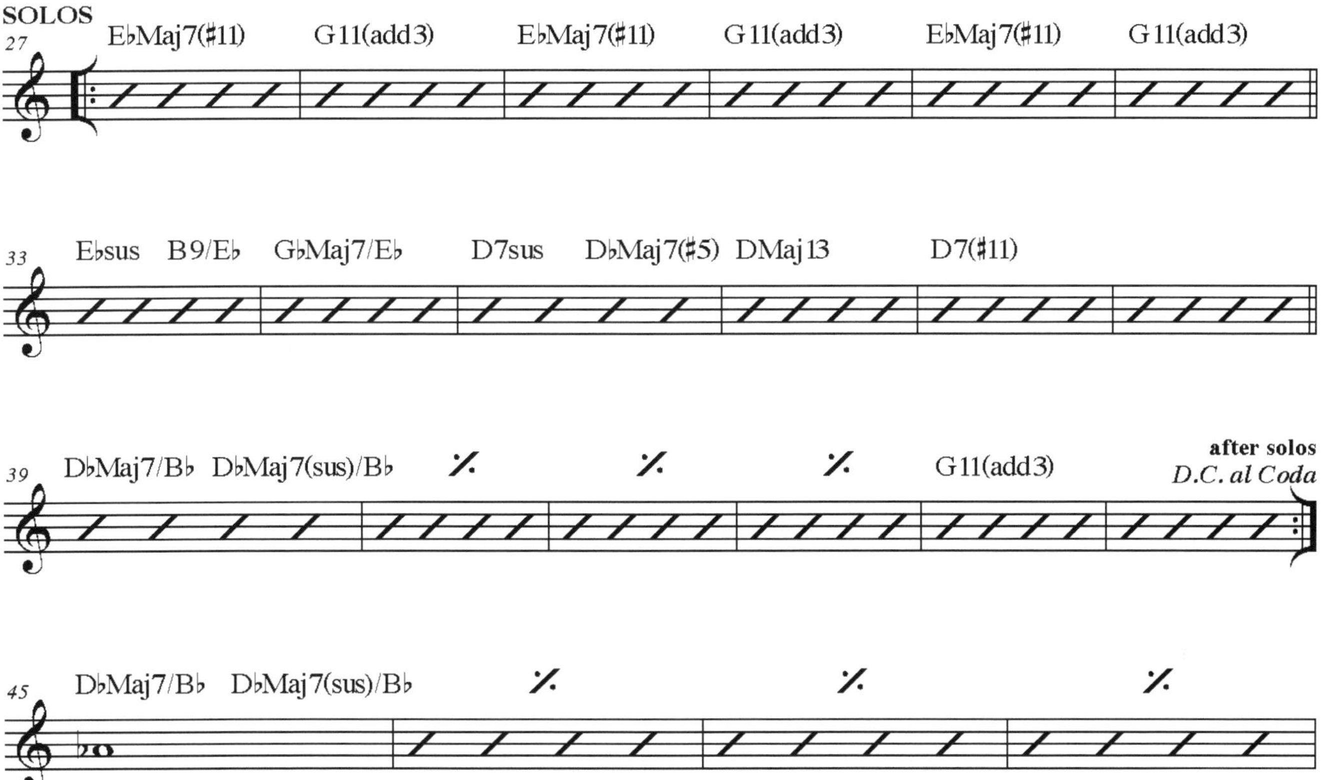

SOLOS
27
EbMaj7(#11)   G11(add3)   EbMaj7(#11)   G11(add3)   EbMaj7(#11)   G11(add3)
33
Ebsus   B9/Eb   GbMaj7/Eb   D7sus   DbMaj7(#5)   DMaj13   D7(#11)
39
DbMaj7/Bb   DbMaj7(sus)/Bb   G11(add3)
after solos
D.C. al Coda

45
DbMaj7/Bb   DbMaj7(sus)/Bb

CODA
49
DbMaj7/Bb   DbMaj7(sus)/Bb   G11(add3)
55
EbMaj13   EbMaj13(#11)   EbMaj6,9   EbMaj13(#11)
2
2
EMaj7(#9)
Fine

21st Century

Mordy Ferber

SOLOS: Free Swing (fast)

After solos: (Guitar only)

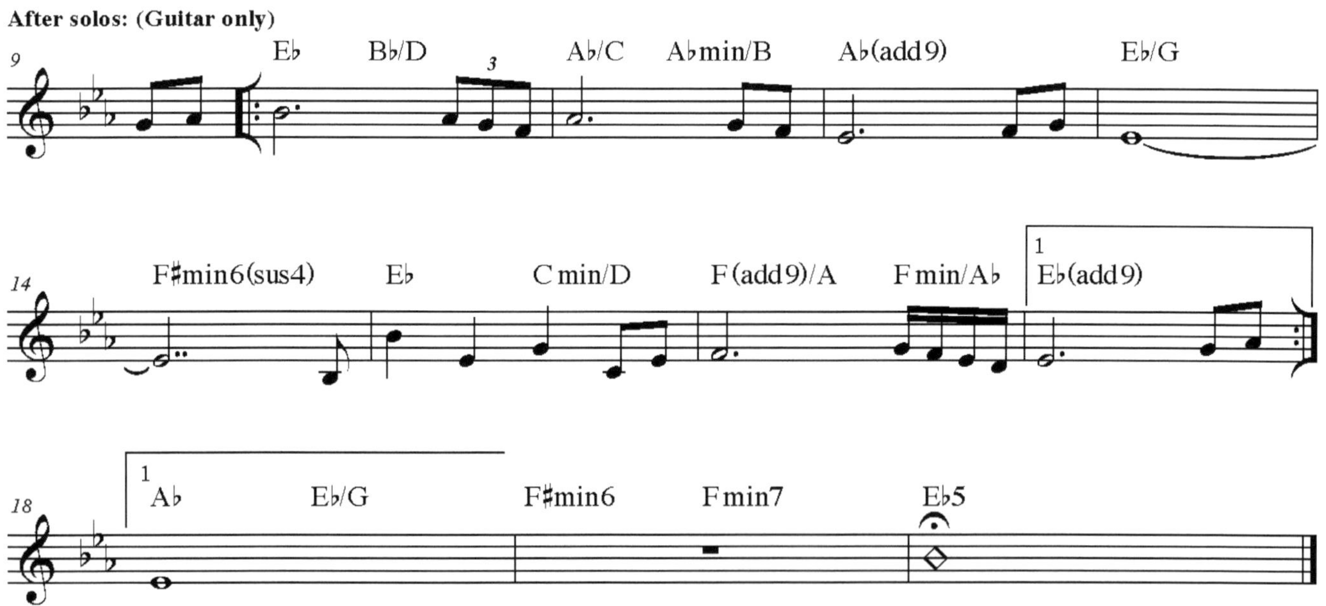

Sole Mate

Mordy Ferber

Sole Mate

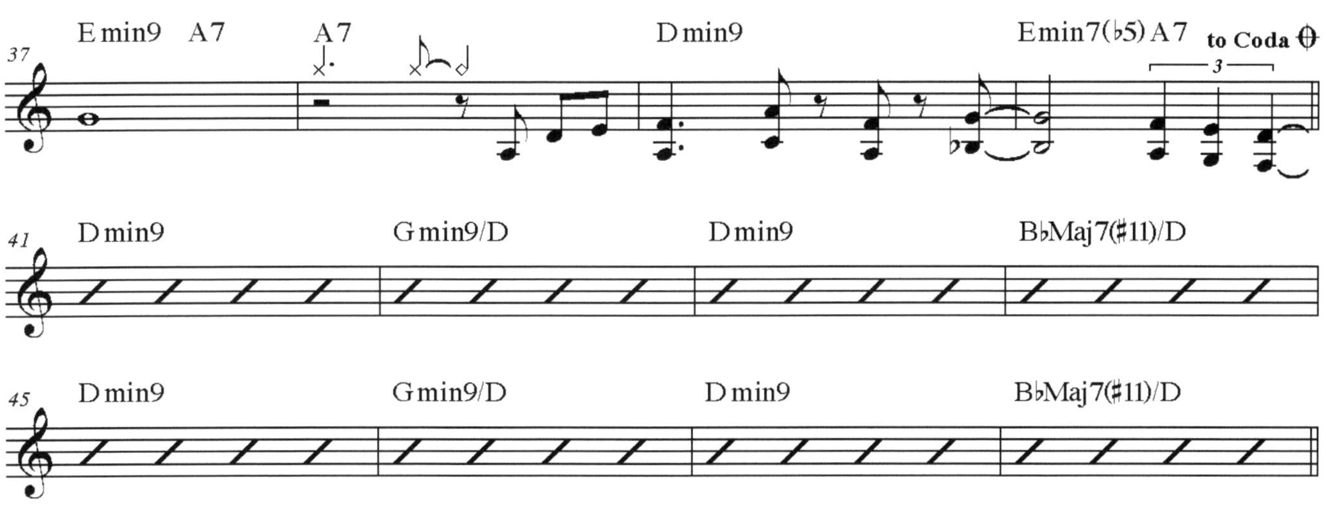

⊕ CODA

B min11

49

A Maj13(♯11)

53

Tuaca

Mordy Ferber

Tuaca

OPEN SOLOS (fast swing)

INTERLUDE (between solos)

BASS SOLO
after solos, *D.S. al Coda*

Warwick

River of Life

Mordy Ferber

River of Life

49
E min7   B min7   E min7   B min7   A min9   B min11/A   A min9   B7(#9) B7(b9)

57
E min7   B min7   E min7   B min7   E min7   B min7   E min7   E min7

65
Cadd9(#11)   E min9

69
Cadd9(#11)

73
B7 Phryg.

77
B7 Phryg.

81
E min7   B min7   E min7   B min7   E min7   B min7   E min7   B min7

89
E min7   B min7   E min7   B min7

White Sand

Mordy Ferber

White Sand
FMaj7 Bmin7 E7 A Bmin7 C#min F#min Bmin A/C# C/D D/E
end solo
B
Eb F/Eb F(add9)/A Bb(add9) BLyd.
BLyd./G Cmin11 F7sus F7 Eb C(add9)/E
F F(add9)/A BLyd. BLyd./G Cmin11 F7sus F7
D.S. al Coda
CODA
C#min F#min Bmin7 A/C# DMaj7 G7sus Eb/Db E/C
A7sus A7sus D Gmin/D D Gmin6/D
D Gmin/D D Gmin6/D D Gmin/D D/F# G/A
A7sus A7sus

Nearly Gone

Mordy Ferber

D
E min9   A min7   G min7   E min9   A min7   G min7
33
E min9   A min7   G min7   E min9   A min7   G min7
37
E
E min9   A min7   G min7   E min9   A min7   G min7
41
E min9   A min7   G min7   E min9   A min7   G min7
45
SOLO 1 (Open)
F#min11   FMaj7(#11)   F#min11
49
FMaj7(#11)   Db7(#9)   CMaj7   G2/B   E/G#   A2/B
55
CMaj7   A min7   B min7
61
SOLO 2 (Open)
E min9   A min7   G min7
65
D.S. al Coda
CODA
E min9   A min7   G min7
67
(Open fade out)

For Shirley

Mordy Ferber

E Drive

Mordy Ferber

E Drive
33 B♭/C
37 A7 A♭7 G7 G♭7 B7(♯9) C7(♯9) C♯7(♯9) C7(♯9) B7(♯9)
41 E min
45 fills
49 E min
53 fills to Coda
57
61 to Solos

68

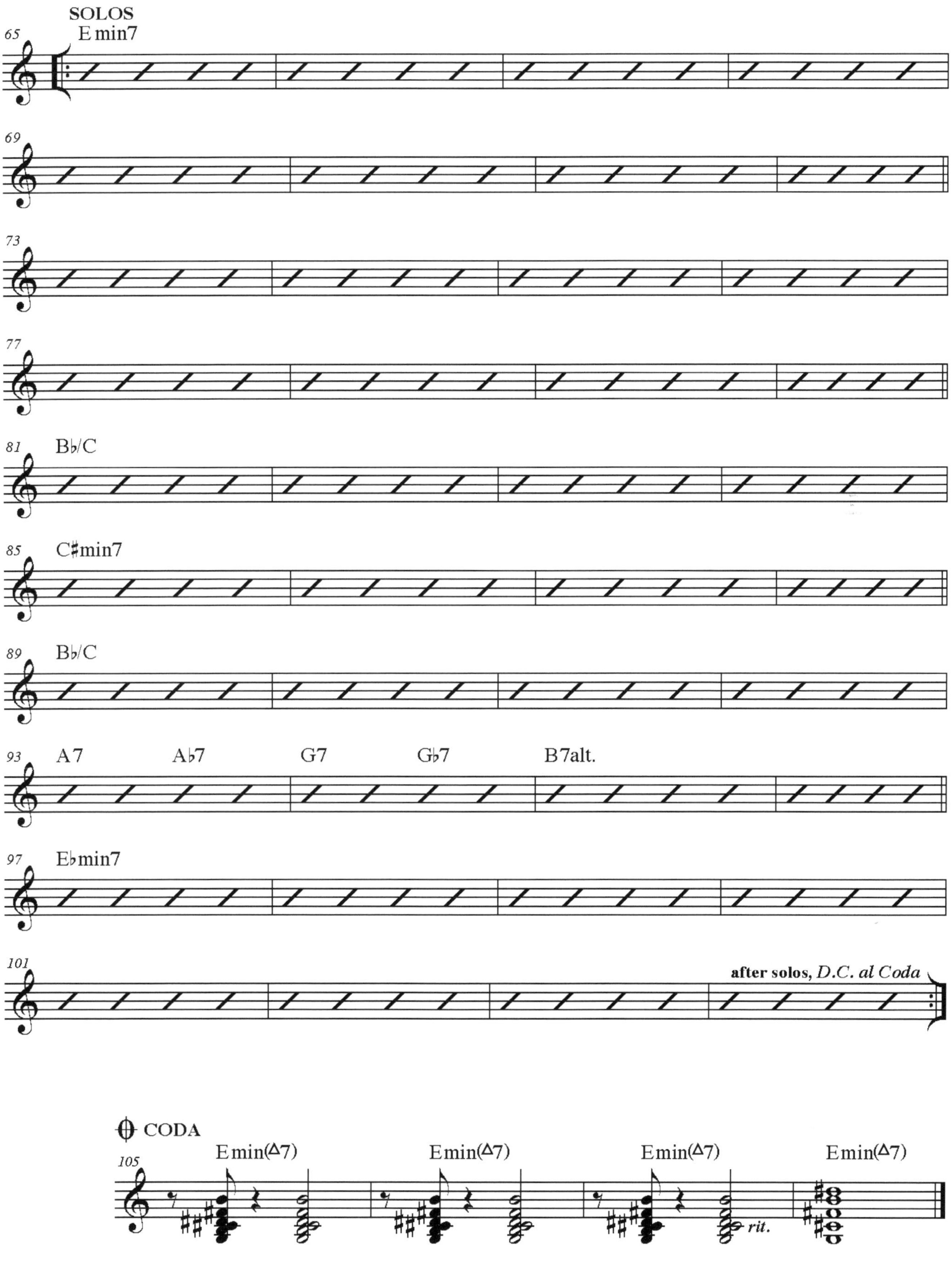

SOLOS
65 Emin7
69
73
77
81 Bb/C
85 C#min7
89 Bb/C
93 A7   Ab7   G7   Gb7   B7alt.
97 Ebmin7
101   after solos, D.C. al Coda
CODA
105 Emin(Δ7)   Emin(Δ7)   Emin(Δ7)   Emin(Δ7)
rit.

Last Call

Mordy Ferber

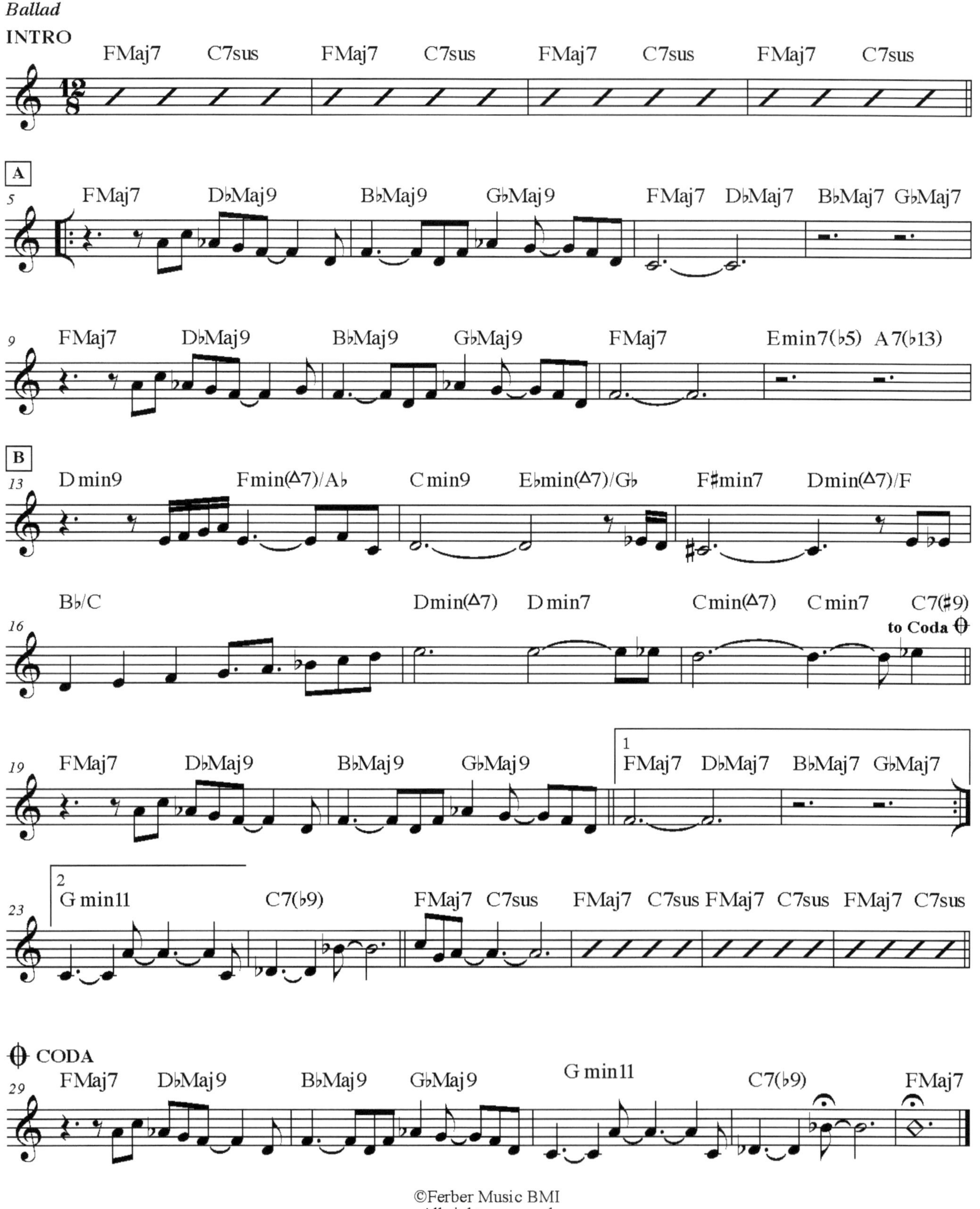

This page has been left blank
to avoid awkward page turns.

Walk of Forgiveness

Mordy Ferber

Walk of Forgiveness

Moving On

Mordy Ferber

30
FMaj7(♯11)
FMaj7(♯11)
rit.
G7sus G13
rit.
B
34
D♭/C C min11
a tempo
3
38
B♭/A A min11
B7(♯9,♭13) Eaug.
to Coda
43
C/A B/A
C/A B♭/A
SOLO (open)
48
A min11
52
G min11
A♭min11
56
A min11
60
G min11
CMaj7(♯5)/E
(On cue:)

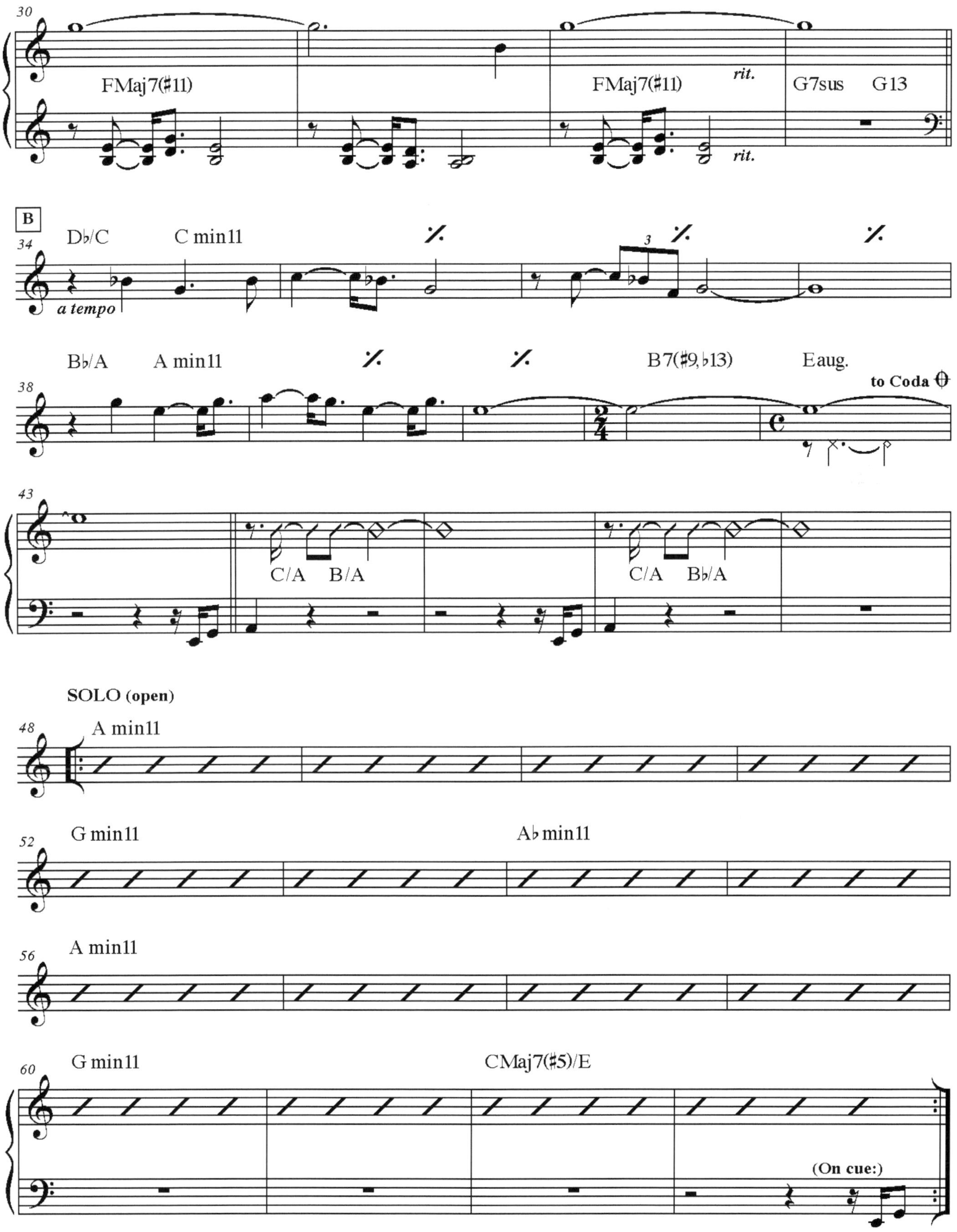

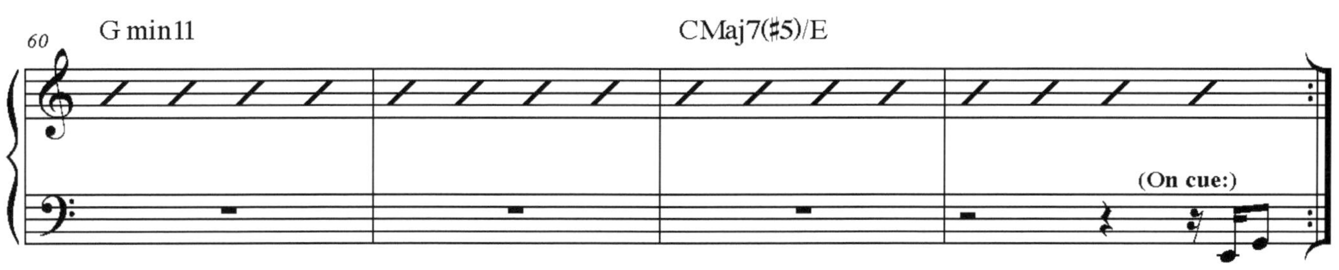

INTERLUDE
after last solo
64
C/A   B/A
C/A   B♭/A
68
D.S. al Coda
C/A   B/A
C/A   B♭/A

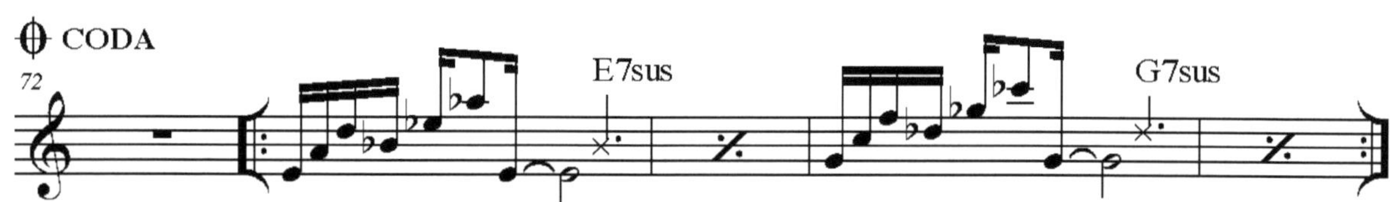

CODA
72
E 7sus
G7sus

77
Fine
E7sus
B min7

This page has been left blank
to avoid awkward page turns.

Piggi's Funk

Mordy Ferber

Piggi's Funk

Piggi's Funk
Cmin7
Fmin7
G7(#9)
A
Cmin7
Fmin7
G7(#9)
Cmin7
Fmin7
G7(#9)
(Fine)
Cmin7
Dmin7
Cmin7
Dmin7
SOLOS (open)
Cmin7
Fmin7
G7(#9)
(last time)
D.S. al Fine
INTERLUDE
Cmin7
Dmin7

Carriage Man

Mordy Ferber

Carriage Man Short

Mordy Ferber

Born in a small town in northern Israel, Mordy Ferber began his musical journey as a singer at the age of 10 performing at school events and small concerts in his hometown. At 12 years of age, after picking up a guitar at the home of a family friend, he decided to take formal guitar lessons. For the following year, he studied with the only teacher available in his town who taught classical music, not his first choice of at that time.

By the time Mordy was a teenager, he was heavily influenced by Rock and was performing covers of Deep Purple, Led Zeppelin, Jimi Hendrix, Cream, the Beatles, and Santana all over Israel. After hearing Django Reinhardt on the radio one day, Mordy was instantly enthralled and his new found love for Django would lead him to discover the likes of Charlie Christian, Joe Pass, Wes Montgomery and Jim Halland Norit Galron, appearing regularly on radio and television shows.

At the age of 18, Mordy joined the Israeli army, a three-year obligation of every Israeli citizen. The first two months were spent in combat training. He soon realized that if he wanted to play the guitar again, he would have to join the army band. Regardless of the music, he preferred a guitar to a gun. For the remainder of his time in the army, he toured the country as part of the military's entertain- ment unit giving concerts to other soldiers in remote areas both inside and out of the country. During this time, Mordy began earning a strong reputation as a guitarist and upon his completion of service, Mordy quickly became one of Israel's top musicians, performing on numerous records for CBS (Sony) with singers like Arik Ainstain, Shlomo Artzi, Shem Tov Levi, Shlomo Gronich, Miki Gavrielov

"It was great training for me, getting so much experience playing in many different styles. I even had the privilege of performing with the legendary Jerry Lewis. At the same time, I continued to work on jazz and developed as an improviser by myself during this period."

At 23, Mordy received a full scholarship to Berklee College of Music in Boston and immigrated to the United States. He graduated in 1987 with full honours and received the prestigious Jim Hall award for outstanding musicianship.

Mordy Ferber has performed and recorded with artists including Michael Brecker, Jack DeJohnette, Eddie Gomez, Peter Erskine, Bob Mintzer, Dave Liebman, Miroslav Vitous, Jeff Berlin, Danny Gottlieb, Bob Moses, Richie Beirach, Richard Bona, George Garzone, Will Lee, Larry Coryell, Adam Nussbaum and Billy Hart. He has recorded 3 albums as a leader on the Enja, Half Note and CBS Europe Record labels.

Mordy has twenty-six years of teaching experience at such prestigious institutions as New York University, Berklee College of Music in Boston, the New School University, American Institute for Guitar and the Sam Ash Institute in New York City. He is highly sought after for his private instruction and has taught master classes in improvisation technique, harmony and composition all over the world. Mordy is regularly commissioned to write music for television and film and his work has been used widely in shows such as the Sopranos, Six Feet Under, Jack Ass, The Tonight Show with Jay Leno, The Guilty on HBO, Fresh Prince, Bay Watch, Felicity, Chris Rock Special on HBO, Everybody Loves Raymond, Veronica's Closet, the VH1 Fashion Award Show, the Grammy Awards promo, and on many other prime time television shows and movies worldwide.

Mordy's playing and compositions defy classification for the simple reason that he emulates no one and does more than his share to bring jazz into the 21st century. Writing expressive music for multiple instruments, he effortlessly joins the intricacies of melody and musicianship. As veteran pianist Richie Beirach explains, "Mordy Ferber is a very individual guitarist/composer. He has distilled the essence of the best musicians of his generation and has come up with a fresh approach within the language of contemporary guitar improvisation." the legendary drummer, Jack DeJohnette says, "I love his sound and his feeling. He writes beautiful compositions. Mordy is committed to the highest level of quality and creativity. He is not afraid to take risks."
Mordy endorses Godin Multiac Nylon & Steel Guitars, Framus Electric Guitars, La Bella guitar strings, Fishman combo acoustic amps and Henriksen JazzAmps.

For more info please go to ***www.mordyferber.com.***

UNIQUELY INTERESTING MUSIC!

Made in the USA
Charleston, SC
02 October 2010